A HANDFUL
OF PEBBLES

A HANDFUL
OF PEBBLES

*Theological Liberalism
and the Church*

Peter Barnes

THE BANNER OF TRUTH TRUST

THE BANNER OF TRUTH TRUST
3 Murrayfield Road, Edinburgh EH12 6EL, UK
P.O. Box 621, Carlisle, PA 17013, USA

First published by Covenanter Press,
NSW 2790, Australia, 2003
First Banner of Truth edition 2008
© Peter Barnes 2008

ISBN-13: 978 0 85151 977 7

Typeset in 11/15 pt Sabon at
the Banner of Truth Trust
Printed in the U.S.A. by
Versa Press, Inc.,
East Peoria, IL

CONTENTS

PUBLISHER'S NOTE

This book was previously published in 2003 as *Theological Liberalism: A Handful of Pebbles* by Covenanter Press of Lithgow, New South Wales, Australia (the publishing arm of the Presbyterian Reformed Church of Australia). It is republished now with only minor editorial changes.

The author, Dr Peter Barnes, is the minister of Revesby Presbyterian Church, Sydney, and lectures in Church History at the Presbyterian Theological Centre in Burwood. He is also the author of *The Milk of the Word: An Introduction to the Christian Faith*, *Both Sides Now: Ecclesiastes and the Human Condition*, *Seeing Jesus*, and *Open Your Mouth for the Dumb*, all published by the Banner of Truth Trust.

It continues to be true, as a prominent liberal theologian acknowledged, that liberal theology offers the seeker after spiritual food only 'a handful of pebbles', while the true gospel holds out to him Jesus Christ, the Bread of Life (*John* 6:35). This book is sent out with the prayer that the God and Father of our Lord Jesus Christ will use it to remove difficulties from the minds of sincere seekers and to feed them with 'the true bread from heaven' which 'gives life to the world' (*John* 6:32–33).

THE PUBLISHER
January 2008

I

WHAT IS THEOLOGICAL LIBERALISM?

At first sight, the word 'liberal' does not seem so threatening. Quite the reverse. It is associated with words like 'democracy' and 'freedom'. Did not the saints in Judea glorify God for the obedience of the Corinthians to the gospel of Christ and for their 'liberal' sharing with them and all men? (2 *Cor.* 9:13, AV, NKJV). The word 'liberal' there sounds like something commendable, and it seems that we should all be liberal. But what the apostle Paul means in that instance is that we should be generous (ESV, NIV). It has nothing to do with theological liberalism.

Liberalism is not a well-defined term, but it is usually taken to refer to a belief system which rejects the orthodox view of the Christian faith as set out in the Bible, and summarized in the historic creeds. The orthodox view of Christianity emphasizes God as the Creator; the Bible as the inerrant Word of God; Christ as the eternal Son of the Father; the crucifixion of Christ as that which pays the sinner's debt to God; Christ's resurrection as the unique and historical defeat of death; the Holy Spirit as the one who makes these things known to us; and heaven and hell as real places which represent the eternal destinies of all who have ever walked this earth.

Theological liberals (or modernists, as they are sometimes called) reject some or all of these beliefs of orthodox Christianity. They usually claim to be objective, and so not biased, in their approach to Scripture. A. S. Peake claimed: 'The Bible is to be studied just like any other book. We can come to it with no prepossessions, but simply with an open mind.' The liberal mind claims to be anti-dogmatic and humanitarian, and for the most part, is not open to the notion of supernatural and infallible divine revelation.

Historic Christianity is often dismissed as not worthy of consideration by any serious seeker. Hence

John Hick takes the high moral ground, and writes: 'Christianity can only remain honestly believable by being continuously open to the truth.' Detached rationalistic neutrality is a decision against faith. For many, indeed most, of these critics, the possibility of God's intervening in history is excluded in the premise; it is not arrived at via objective methods in order to reach a scientific conclusion. God is closed out of the equation before the sums are added up.

Christianity claims to be supernatural. In fact, everything in it is supernatural – the creation itself, God's providential care of the world, miracles, the judgment at the end, even the person of Christ himself. David Hume (1711–76) – to cite one critic – rejects this whole approach, and so writes of miracles: 'A miracle is a violation of the laws of nature; and as a firm and unalterable experience has established these laws, the proof against a miracle, from the very nature of the fact, is as entire as any argument from experience can possibly be imagined.' Hume has missed the obvious point that by definition there can be no miracles unless there are laws which are transcended by a supernatural intervention. His statement is not so much an argument as an assertion.

Hume's world view simply excluded the possibility of miracles. In fact, any kind of evidence of supernaturalism is discarded as something which does not happen. Such dogmatic scepticism is not uncommon, although it usually hides behind scientific-sounding phrases. Howard Kee even claims that the miracles were never intended to be understood as historical events but only as symbols. But symbolic cures and feedings neither delight nor upset the general populace.

Sometimes, liberals confront the Bible head-on; sometimes they adopt a more beguiling stance. For example, one often hears of a desire for a plurality of theologies today, supposedly to enrich the Church. J. D. G. Dunn writes in this way, arguing that there were a number of different theologies at work even within the New Testament itself. Frances Young writes in the same vein: 'To recognise the possibility that diverse responses to Jesus Christ have equal validity may well be the only constructive way forward in a world which is beginning to value the enriching aspects of its variety and pluralism.' She wrote this in a volume entitled, *The Myth of God Incarnate*! But if words mean anything, and if there is any logic left in the world, it is difficult to see how one who admires Jesus as a great man is doing something just as valid as the one who bows before him as Lord and God.

Ideas have consequences. Ultimately, they will motivate governments, move armies, and pull down empires. If people believe that God has spoken his unsullied truth in the Bible, that will affect how they live. If they do not believe that the Bible is high truth, that too will affect how they live.

It is important to distinguish between a matter of interpretation and a matter of authority. Christians have always differed over secondary issues (see *Rom.* 14:1). For example, one Christian may believe that only believers should be baptized while another may believe that children too are included in God's covenant with his people. That is a matter of interpretation. Unanimity on all matters will only happen in heaven.

However, differences are sometimes presented in a way designed to trap the unwary. For example, in the debate over whether or not women can be pastors in the church, it is common to hear that it is a matter of the interpretation of Scripture. In some cases that may be true, but often it is not a matter of interpretation but of authority. Those who favour women pastors invariably dislike texts such as 1 Corinthians 11:3 and 1 Timothy 2:11–15, and so explain them away. Christ is betrayed not with a frontal assault but with an interpretation.

2

WARNINGS IN THE BIBLE

It is instructive that the Bible gives so much time and space to warning God's people about the dangers of false teaching. Some of these warnings concern the pursuit of gods other than the Lord who reveals himself in Scripture (*Deut.* 13:1–5), while other warnings tell of false prophets who come in the name of the true God (*Deut.* 18:20–22). Elijah and Elisha lived in the 9th century B.C. and battled hard against the prophets of Baal. But there were other prophets – a majority in fact – who simply told the king of Israel exactly what he wanted to hear (see *1 Kings* 22). This was the ancient equivalent of being fawned upon by the religious department of the BBC.

In those dark days when the Babylonians threatened Jerusalem, and then destroyed the city and the temple, the prophets Jeremiah and Ezekiel especially confronted false prophets who preached a soft and superficial peace based on positive thinking without repentance (*Jer.* 5:31; 23:9–40; 28:1–17; *Ezek.* 13:1–23). Earlier, the prophet Micah had been faced with the same kind of false teaching which treated sin lightly (*Mic.* 2:6–3:12). Later, Nehemiah was to be troubled by a false prophetess (*Neh.* 6:14). False teaching, which went hand-in-hand with false living, was a recurring temptation for God's ancient people.

Nor is the story any different in the New Testament. Our Lord himself warns against false prophets who come in sheep's clothing but inwardly are ravenous wolves (*Matt.* 7:15–20). Not only will there be false Christs (Messiahs), but false prophets will deceive many (*Matt.* 24:5,11). Faith is nowhere equated with gullibility or the acceptance of the latest offering from the theological seminary.

In the early church there were those within her ranks who taught that Christ's work was not enough for salvation; it was necessary to add circumcision to what Christ did at Calvary (*Acts* 15:1). Such an error called forth the Apostle Paul's sternest condemnation: 'But even if we or an angel from heaven should preach to you a gospel contrary to the one we preached to you, let him be accursed' (*Gal.* 1:8). In case we missed what Paul was saying he repeats it in the next verse (*Gal.* 1:9).

When Paul spoke to the elders of the Ephesian church, he warned of fierce wolves who would come in among them and lead professing Christians astray (*Acts* 20:29–30). The church at Corinth was ravaged by preachers who told of another Jesus, a different spirit, and a different gospel (2 *Cor.* 11:4). Paul's warning is quite explicit:

> For such men are false apostles, deceitful workmen, disguising themselves as apostles of Christ. And no wonder, for even Satan disguises himself as an angel of light. So it is no surprise if his servants, also, disguise themselves as servants of righteousness. Their end will correspond to their deeds (2 *Cor.* 11:13–15).

Christians face a constant danger of being led away from the sufficiency of Christ and back into empty philosophies and the shadows of reality (*Gal.* 5:2, 4; *Col.* 2:8–10). To add to the work of Christ is to undo it. It is easy to be deceived (2 *Thess.* 2:3; *1 Tim.* 4:1–5). Men who once led the church may fall into serious error (*1 Tim.* 1:18–20; 2 *Tim.* 2:16–18;

4:10). A faithful elder needs to be able to contradict those who reject God's truth (*Titus* 1:9).

At the end of the epistle to the Romans, Paul writes warmly of Christian brothers and sisters – he mentions twenty-six of them by name – who had helped him or had fellowship with him in the cause of Christ. Then all of a sudden, Paul's attention is diverted to false teachers who, if Douglas Moo's suggestion is right, may have been on their way to Rome. Paul writes vehemently:

> I appeal to you, brothers, to watch out for those who cause divisions and create obstacles contrary to the doctrine that you have been taught; avoid them. For such persons do not serve our Lord Christ, but their own appetites, and by smooth talk and flattery they deceive the hearts of the naive (*Rom.* 16:17–18).

False teachers were a problem in the life of the early church, and they have continued to plague the church ever since.

The Apostle Peter warns of false teachers who secretly (hardly ever openly) bring in destructive heresies and become slaves to corruption (2 *Pet.* 2). Such persons, says Jude, are

> waterless clouds, swept along by winds; fruitless trees in late autumn, twice dead, uprooted; wild waves

of the sea, casting up the foam of their own shame; wandering stars, for whom the gloom of utter darkness has been reserved for ever (*Jude* 12–13).

In short, they do not have the Holy Spirit (*Jude* 19).

The 'apostle of love', John, also warns the believer with these cautionary words:

> Beloved, do not believe every spirit, but test the spirits to see whether they are from God, for many false prophets have gone out into the world (*1 John* 4:1).

We are not to have fellowship with someone who denies the basic truths of the gospel; we are to do nothing that may give the impression that we are one with such a person (*2 John* 9–11). John is not afraid to name Diotrephes, a prominent church leader of his day, who was nevertheless proudly despising those who held to the apostolic gospel (*3 John* 9–11).

Christians are to 'contend earnestly for the faith which was once for all delivered to the saints' (*Jude* 3). Churches which remain firm to the apostolic teaching and life are commended by the Lord (*Rev.* 2:6, 24). Those which capitulate to worldly error are held worthy of blame and rebuke (*Rev.* 2:14–15, 20–23). There is a false prophet who will lead many to worship the beast which relies on worldly power, but God will judge and damn forever those who pit themselves against his divine authority (*Rev.* 13:11–18; 20:10).

Arthur W. Pink, writing at a time when so many within the church were turning away from the historic Christian faith, said with his typical boldness: 'The apostles of Satan are not saloon-keepers and white-slave traffickers, but are for the most part ordained ministers.' A painful reality we need to grasp is that not all who speak in the name of Christ are true Christians who proclaim the 'truth as it is in Jesus'. It might be stating the obvious, but false teachers never announce themselves as such.

Since by nature we have what Paul calls 'itching ears', we can so easily find excuses to reject sound doctrine (2 *Tim.* 4:3–4). Loving God with our mind as well as with heart, soul, and strength, we are to 'test everything; (and) hold fast what is good' (*1 Thess.* 5:21). In what proved to be his last epistle, Second Timothy – a kind of last will and testament – Paul wrote: 'Follow the pattern of the sound words that you have heard from me, in the faith and love that are in Christ Jesus' (2 *Tim.* 1:13).

When he was enthroned as Archbishop of Canterbury in 1980, Robert Runcie declared: 'The Church must give a firm lead against rigid thinking.' Runcie certainly did that – indeed, Runcie was often an implacable opponent of any kind of thinking!

However, it is not easy to reconcile his approach with that of the Apostle Paul. Writing again to his 'beloved child' in the faith, Timothy, he solemnly said: 'I charge you in the presence of God and of Christ Jesus, who is to judge the living and the dead, and by his appearing and his kingdom: preach the word' (2 *Tim.* 4:1–2).

3

A BRIEF HISTORY OF
THE RISE OF LIBERALISM

There have always been people who say they are Christians but who scoff at Christian teaching. In the second century, Marcion cut out verses from the New Testament that implied any kind of acceptance of the Old Testament, especially with regard to its teachings on the creation of the physical world and the giving of the law. As his opponent Tertullian said, Marcion would 'rather call a passage an addition than explain it'. He preferred the use of the knife to that of the pen. Marcion was excommunicated by the church in A.D. 144, but since that time he has had many theological successors, especially in the modern period; and it is in theological seminaries that many of them can be found.

Kenneth Scott Latourette referred to the nineteenth century as the 'Great Century'. In many ways it was great; but it was also a time when biblical criticism, which had developed in the eighteenth century, became more pervasive in many of the Protestant churches. Hence A. N. Wilson, citing Thomas Hardy, refers to this period as 'God's funeral'.

In 1836 Thomas Carlyle said that the age was 'at once destitute of faith and terrified at scepticism'. By 1873 Matthew Arnold could speak of 'a change in religion as great as that which happened at the Reformation'. The mood of the age was indeed captured by Matthew Arnold in his poem *Dover Beach*:

> The sea of faith
> Was once, too, at the full, and round earth's shore
> Lay like the folds of a bright girdle furl'd;
> But now I only hear
> Its melancholy long withdrawing roar,
> Retreating . . .

The second half of the nineteenth century was a world between two times.

One of the first modern biblical critics was Richard Simon (1638–1712) who, as a Roman Catholic, argued that since the Bible was fallible, Protestantism had no clear authority. Protestants should therefore return to the infallible authority of Rome. Since then, liberalism has entered the Roman Catholic Church too, despite the encyclical of Pope Leo XIII (1893) which declared, 'All the books and the whole of each book which the Church receives as sacred and canonical were written at the dictation of the Holy Spirit.'

Germany in the eighteenth and nineteenth centuries witnessed a flourishing of 'Enlightenment' thinking. The leading figures in this movement were Immanuel Kant (1724–1804), G. E. Lessing (1729–81), Johann Wolfgang von Goethe (1749–1832), Georg Hegel (1770–1831), and Friedrich Schleiermacher (1768–1834). Lessing asserted that there was an 'ugly broad ditch' between reason and history. By this, he meant that no historical truth could be demonstrated. Since Christianity is a religion based upon firm historical events – for example, the Creation, the Exodus, Jesus' own death and resurrection – faith could only maintain a tenuous link with history and so with reason. Religion was portrayed as something of an irrational leap in the dark. Reality is rational, that is, it exists without any supernatural intervention. God might exist, but he is out of the equation, as it were.

Kant saw limits to reason, and he divorced faith from the scientific and historical realm. The Frenchman René Descartes, on the other hand, held to reason alone. Schleiermacher then tried to ground faith in human experience and feeling, and divorce it from reason and history. The resultant liberal faith was the theological equivalent of John Keats's Romanticism: 'I am certain of nothing except the holiness of the heart's affections, and the truth of the imagination.' This made for confusion, as professing believers lurched back and forth between the claims of rationalism and irrationalism.

In 1893 T. K. Cheyne referred to J. G. Eichhorn (1752–1827) as 'the founder of modern Old Testament criticism'. Eichhorn came to vague views on the authority of the Bible, and indulged in much historical reconstruction of it. In a revealing comment, the *Oxford Dictionary of the Christian Church* says of him: 'His work, though inaccurate, was popular and did much to encourage Biblical study and criticism.' Not many people can expect to be applauded in life for being inaccurate.

It was not long before these German ideas came, by various means, to Great Britain and began to influence men like Samuel Taylor Coleridge (1772–1834), Thomas Arnold (1795–1842), Canon Thirlwall (1797–1875), Julius Hare (1795–1855), and F. D. Maurice (1805–72). The year 1860 saw the publication of *Essays and Reviews,* in which seven prominent scholars, mostly from Oxford, cast doubt on the verbal inspiration of Scripture and the doctrine of everlasting punishment. It is instructive that the questioning of hell had little to do with the supposed science of biblical criticism. It was simply that people revolted at the doctrine of a punishment that lasts forever. Charles Darwin was one who referred to everlasting punishment as 'a damnable doctrine'. In the midst of the turmoil, the Anglican bishops hesitated to act against the seven authors, and inaction helped to encourage the further spread of liberalism.

The publication of *Essays and Reviews* was a watershed. It was followed by Bishop Colenso's rejection of the Mosaic authorship of the Pentateuch (the first five books of the Bible), and by Charles Gore's collection of essays entitled *Lux Mundi,* published in 1889, in which he argued that Christ was mistaken in regarding the Old Testament as the infallible Word of God.

The new views soon spread to the United States of America. Charles A. Briggs (1844–1913) of Union Theological Seminary in New York tended to be quite evangelical in his theological views – for example, he declared that he believed in the Virgin

Birth – but he denied the inerrancy of Scripture. When Briggs was found guilty of heresy by the Presbyterian Church of the United States of America in 1891, Union Theological Seminary responded to this act of church discipline by cutting its ties with the denomination in 1892. The Assembly responded by suspending Briggs.

In Roman Catholic circles, modernism emerged with the teaching of men such as Edouard Le Roy (1870–1954), Alfred Loisy (1857–1940) and George Tyrrell (1861–1909). In 1910 Pope Pius X responded to the rising challenge by imposing an anti-modernist oath on all priests. Le Roy formally submitted, but Loisy and Tyrrell refused, and were excommunicated. Since Vatican II (1962–5), Roman Catholic theologians have increasingly rejected biblical infallibility, and embraced some form of liberalism or modernism.

A rough kind of chronology is observable in the rise of liberal theology in the modern period. In general, the Old Testament was questioned first, then the writings of the Apostle Paul, and finally Christ himself was portrayed in a way which differed radically from the eye-witness accounts of the New Testament writers.

THE OLD TESTAMENT

German scholars in particular attacked the authority of the Old Testament. One of the earliest liberals, Friedrich Schleiermacher, refused to preach from the Old Testament. Two of the earliest Old Testament critics, W. M. L. de Wette (1780–1849) and Wilhelm Gesenius (1786–1843) were both prone to dismiss as 'Jewish' any part of the Old Testament to which they objected. Much of the Old Testament record was thought to be of little historical value. The philosopher Johann Gottlieb Fichte (1762–1814), who studied Protestant theology at university, was probably the first to suggest that Jesus was not a Jew but an Aryan.

Prophecies are by definition supernatural, and so they were quick to fall under suspicion. Christian Carl Josias von Bunsen (1791–1860), for example, claimed that Isaiah 9:1–7 referred to the birth of Hezekiah (despite the fact that the child is called 'the mighty God'!) and also that Isaiah 53 referred to Jeremiah, who was supposed to have been stoned in Egypt (apparently thereby bearing 'the iniquity of us all').

The speculations of Charles Darwin (1809–82) meant that Genesis 1–11 came to be interpreted as symbol or poetry rather than straightforward history. Despite the fact that transition animals between species were (and continue to be) missing from the fossil record, Darwin postulated that one species evolved into another over millions of years. In 1859 he published his notorious book *On the Origin of Species*. He came to see life as driven by the tautologous notions of natural selection and survival of the fittest. He compared apes and human 'savages', and concluded that the difference between man and the higher animals is one of degree, not kind. Indeed, the hesitant and restrained Darwin still prophesied:

> Looking to the world at no very distant date, what an endless number of the lower races will have been eliminated by the higher civilized races throughout the world.

Eugenics and the master race theory were the next logical steps along this darkened road.

It was not long too long before the church accepted the theory of evolution. True, in 1861 Bishop Samuel Wilberforce of Oxford (known as 'Soapy Sam') did famously debate the issue with T. H. Huxley (known as 'Darwin's Bulldog'), but in Britain a truce between the warring factions was soon declared. Robert Rainy in 1874 declared that evolution and theology were 'perfectly at ease'. Inevitably, the venerable, biblical, and realistic doctrine of original sin had to be toned down to fit in with evolution's more optimistic view of human nature. No longer was the church willing to sing with Isaac Watts:

> Alas! And did my Saviour bleed?
> And did my Sovereign die?
> Would He devote that sacred head
> For such a worm as I?

Samuel Angus (1881–1943) of the Presbyterian Church of Australia, was even to say that Genesis 3 had to be interpreted as a 'fall' upwards, for it resulted in moral consciousness!

Henry Drummond (1851–97) from the Free Church College in Glasgow evangelized with D. L. Moody and also campaigned for the acceptance of biblical criticism and of evolution. To Drummond, a lovable and pious-sounding man, both the spiritual world and the natural world were evolving – which meant that he could not adhere to the faith delivered once for all to the saints. In fact, Drummond's definition of a Christian was 'a man who furthers the evolution of the world according to the purposes of Jesus Christ'.

In 1878, the year of what William Henry Green called 'the sudden revolution', Julius Wellhausen (1844–1918) published his theory that Israel's prophets came before the law, despite the Bible's teaching to the contrary. He asserted that the Pentateuch (Genesis–Deuteronomy) was the result of the late gathering together of four documents – labelled J, E, D, and P – which were written many centuries apart and had widely differing views of God. According to his theory, an enterprising editor pasted together these documents, one of which referred to God as Jehovah (the J document), another as Elohim (the E document); and then added Deuteronomy (the D document, supposedly written in the days of Josiah, not Moses) and the Priestly document (P, supposedly written in the 6th century B.C., again not by Moses but partly by Ezekiel). In one sense, the Bible of the critics was a more miraculous work than the Bible of evangelical believers! Wellhausen, however, did at least recognize that it was dishonest for him to prepare ministerial students for the Protestant Church.

In a very detailed work, published between 1862 and 1879, J. W. Colenso (1814–83), Bishop of

Natal, cast great doubt on the historicity of the first six books of the Old Testament. In some 3,500 pages he suggested that Ezekiel had written Leviticus 18–27, and that Jeremiah was probably the author of Deuteronomy. He even suggested that the Passover was originally a spring festival of the sun-god, which included child sacrifice. Not surprisingly, Colenso did not accept the historicity of the Bible's miracles. He came to believe that 'the pure in heart' would recognize those parts of the Bible where God revealed himself. Colenso's speculations led him to embrace universalism, the comforting doctrine that everyone will be saved in the end.

William Robertson Smith (1846–94) proceeded from his own theological studies to become Professor of Hebrew in the Free Church College at Aberdeen in 1870. He endeavoured to popularize the Wellhausen theories of the Old Testament, and held to the idea that one could preserve evangelical piety while at the same time accepting the assured results of Higher Criticism. Hence he wrote: 'No criticism can take away from us our personal fellowship with God in Christ – no criticism can withdraw from the Bible its living power as the medium wherein we are brought face to face with Christ; for a personal faith lies too deep to be touched by criticism.'

These soothing words were devoid of common sense. Biblical faith is based on biblical history. If God did not create the world, if he did not redeem Israel from Egypt, if Christ did not die and rise from the dead, the church's theology has no sure foundation. Yet so many professing Christians at the time did not see the danger. T. K. Cheyne even wrote *Aids to the Devout Study of Criticism*! Thomas Carlyle was more hard-headed: 'Have my countrymen's heads become turnips when they think that they can hold the premises of German unbelief and draw the conclusions of Scottish Evangelical Orthodoxy?'

After a long and drawn-out dispute, Smith was deposed in 1881, but it was clear that the new critical views he espoused were being accepted. S. R. Driver, who was more moderate than many of his fellow critics, succeeded the conservative Anglo-Catholic E. B. Pusey at Oxford in 1882, and published his *Introduction to the Literature of the Old Testament* in 1891. For Driver, the Bible's understanding of history and science could be criticized, but not its spiritual and moral truths. The prophets apparently knew more about heaven than they did about the earth.

It became commonplace to embrace what was regarded as 'critical orthodoxy'. Genesis 1–11 was viewed as mythology, pre-historic legend, or poetry; Genesis 1 was not science and Genesis 3 was not history; Genesis–Deuteronomy consisted of four documents dated many centuries apart, which were fused together by an unknown editor; the book of Isaiah arose from the writings of two or possibly three prophets; and the book of Daniel belonged to the second century rather than the sixth century B.C. Many of the Psalms were dated much later than the time of King David – not that the Bible says that he wrote all of them.

Despite the fact that in Matthew 22:41–46, Christ used the Davidic authorship of Psalm 110 to point out that the Messiah was both David's Lord and his son, liberals consistently maintained, without much evidence, that David could not have written this Psalm, nor many others.

PAUL

The rejection of Paul and the other apostles is crucial, because Jesus himself never wrote anything. We only know him through the writings of the apostles, those eye-witnesses of his life and work. To put it bluntly, if they were wrong about Jesus, we have no real and reliable access to him.

Ferdinand Christian Baur (1792–1860) and the Tübingen school portrayed early Christianity as a battle between two factions – with the liberal Paul on the one hand opposing the more conservative Peter, James, and the Jerusalem church on the other. This conflict was blurred by the resultant synthesis in the book of Acts which produced an unhistorical early Catholicism, reconciling the two factions. He also argued that the Gospel of Mark was written in the second century, although most contemporary scholarship regards it as the first of the four Gospels to be composed. Baur's interpretation owed more to Hegel's view of history than it did to any sober reading of the New Testament.

Wilhelm Wrede (1859–1906) called Paul 'the second founder of Christianity', indeed as one who exerted the stronger, though not the better, influence. Wrede saw the New Testament as just another piece of ancient literature. He claimed that 'no New Testament writing was born with the predicate "canonical" attached'. In Wrede's view, Jesus never claimed to be the Messiah. It was the early church which claimed this for him.

Alfred Rosenberg, one of the thinkers behind National Socialism, attacked the churches for being Pauline rather than Christian. He thought that Paul

Judaized the gospel. German liberal theology – a kind of theological anti-Semitism – helped pave the way for Hitler and the coming to power of a fierce anti-Semitism.

The outlandish views of Baur and his ilk should have been laid to rest by the work of the Cambridge trio, J. B. Lightfoot (1828–89), B. F. Westcott (1825–1901) and F. J. A. Hort (1828–92). Lightfoot, in particular, showed that a late dating of the New Testament was impossible. In this he was supported by the work of the distinguished British archaeologist, Sir William Mitchell Ramsay (1851–1939).

CHRIST HIMSELF

Hermann Samuel Reimarus (1694–1768) wrote a life of Jesus which portrayed the Messiah as a political rebel who performed no real miracles, and who did not expect to die. The disciples stole his body, then waited for fifty days, before spreading the story that Jesus had risen from the dead. This was how the disciples reinterpretated the Messianic hope.

Heinrich Paulus (1761–1851) became professor of theology at Heidelberg University. A bitter anti-

Semite, he praised the holy purity of Jesus' character. However, Paulus explained away all the miracles. When Jesus calmed the storm, it was only because the boat passed by a hill which protected it from the wind. The dead who were raised were only in a deep trance. On the cross, Jesus never actually died, but was revived by the cool air in the tomb, and the earthquake conveniently rolled away the stone so that he could appear resurrected. The Jesus created by Paulus is portrayed as the pinnacle of humanity, but he allowed his followers to believe in his miracles when, according to Paulus, nothing supernatural had occurred at all.

J. S. Semler (1725–91) claimed that Jesus accommodated his real enlightened views to the primitive ideas of his hearers. The real Jesus, it seems, was rather like a cultured liberal preacher with a following of fundamentalist red-necks – a precursor of *Elmer Gantry*.

A former pastor, David Friedrich Strauss (1808-74) wrote a *Life of Jesus* but with the supernatural parts removed. Although well-written, his massive work of over 1,400 pages, presented the Gospel story in terms of mythology. Jesus was presented as 'nothing more than a person, highly distinguished indeed, but subject to the limitations of all that is mortal'. Strauss's presupposition was, in his own words, that 'no supernaturalism shall be suffered to remain'. The historical Jesus was not allowed to be supernatural. However, these novel religious beliefs brought Strauss little comfort. After divorcing his wife, he became obsessed with politics, the Franco-Prussian War, and Darwinism.

Ernst Renan (1823–92) did something similar. A Frenchman, Renan studied for the priesthood until he discovering German critical theology. In 1863 he wrote a *Life of Jesus* in which Jesus is portrayed as a sentimental and idyllic carpenter who threw off the gloomy influence of John the Baptist and went on to preach gentleness and mildness, all the time riding about on a donkey with long eyelashes! Smothering Jesus with sentimental compliments, Renan declared that the Sermon on the Mount was charming. (C. S. Lewis, on the other hand, asked: 'Who can like being knocked flat on his face by a sledge-hammer?') When Jesus came to die, Renan waxed eloquent: 'Rest now, amid Thy glory, noble pioneer.'

Albrecht Ritschl (1822–89) presented the liberal view of Jesus in its most modern and beguiling form. He taught that Jesus reveals the worth of God to us, but he was indifferent to any teaching that Jesus is in his essential being God. He reveals the Fatherhood of

God, and provides us with the example of self-sacrificing love. Adolf von Harnack (1851–1930) taught a similarly simple gospel, with a distrust of doctrine and metaphysics. According to Harnack, this meant that Jesus revealed the Father in some way, but not much more could be said about his relationship with the Father. Harnack's gospel may have been simple, but it was not the biblical gospel. A man who reveals God is one thing, but God becoming man is quite another.

These attempts to get back to the 'historical Jesus', who was by definition human and not divine, led to some bizarre explanations of Jesus' words and deeds. Jesus was supposed to be walking on a sand bar when he was thought to be walking on water; he did not actually feed the five thousand but shamed them into sharing their lunches which they had hidden in their cloaks; and the Apostle John was said to have become so drunk at the wedding feast at Cana that he thought a miracle had taken place when it had not.

In actual fact, Jesus' miracles were so public, so numerous, and so incapable of being explained away that his enemies never thought to deny that he had done them. Instead, they claimed that he performed them using the power of Satan (*Mark* 3:22; see too *John* 11:45–57; *Acts* 4:13–22).

The so-called history-of-religions school, exemplified by the likes of Wilhelm Bousset (1865–1920), Richard Reitzenstein (1861–1931), and Samuel Angus (1881–1943), thought that Christianity was influenced by the Hellenistic cults. The Apostle Paul is supposed to have come across pagan lords, of which there were many (see *1 Cor.* 8:5–6), and thought that the title 'Lord' was worth borrowing for his own purposes. We are meant to believe that this was how Jesus came to be adored as Lord in the full and absolute sense of being a divine ruler. Alas for this neat theory, Jesus is presented as Lord in the Gospels (e.g. *Matt.* 7:21–23; *John* 13:13–15). As Lord, he will decide the eternal destiny of every last human being on the earth. Furthermore, the use of the Aramaic word *Maranatha* ('Come, Lord') in a letter to a Greek church shows that it must have been used back in Palestine (*1 Cor.* 16:22).

Bruno Bauer (1809-1882) reached the limit of this kind of criticism when he finally concluded that there was no historical Jesus. Bereft of any sense of modesty, Bauer considered that he had settled the question for all time! Others followed suit. P. W. Schmiedel (1851–1935) even announced: 'It would not make any difference to my faith were it to turn out that Jesus never lived.' Not so the Apostle Paul, who believed that of first importance to gospel faith was the truth that Jesus Christ had died for sinners and risen again according to the Scriptures (*1 Cor.* 15:3–4). For a person not to believe in these historical facts is to be in a most pitiable condition (*1 Cor.* 15:19).

In 1901 Albert Schweitzer (1875–1965) showed that the quest for the historical Jesus had simply reproduced a Jesus in its own image. To paraphrase George Tyrell, each scholar saw his own reflection at the bottom of the well, and called it 'Jesus'. Schweitzer was a wonderful musician, and became a devoted missionary doctor, but his forays into theology and history leave much to be desired. Schweitzer's own attempt is no more helpful or convincing, for he portrayed a Jesus who mistakenly tried to usher in the end times but instead perished on the cross. No matter, said Schweitzer, for what is important is not the historical Jesus but 'Jesus as spiritually arisen within men'.

Even those who were far more biblical and evangelical than the liberals were often reluctant to press the point and insist that the full-orbed evangelical faith be upheld. James Denney in 1909 declared that the church must bind its members to what he called 'the Christian attitude to Christ', but he added that 'it has no right to bind them to anything else'. In Canada in 1927 Rev. Richard Roberts stated: 'I propose to be both a traditionalist and a modernist.'

4

THE AMERICAN FUNDAMENTALIST CONTROVERSY

In the United Kingdom and Australia, as well as in Europe, some form of liberalism dominated the leadership and the theological seminaries of the mainstream Protestant churches by the outbreak of World War 1. The situation in the U.S.A., however, was a little different. Following the end of World War 1, there was a vigorous renewal of the fundamentalist/modernist controversy. The 12-volume work, *The Fundamentals,* written by sixty-four authors, was published between 1910 and 1915. The work sought to bolster the evangelical cause. Yet, in spite of this great effort, the tide of scholarly opinion was running in the opposite direction.

On 21 May 1922, the liberal Baptist, Harry Emerson Fosdick, preached a provocative sermon, 'Shall the Fundamentalists Win?', from the pulpit of the First Presbyterian Church in New York City. Fosdick's liberalism led him to declare that he believed in the divinity both of Christ and of his own mother! In the ensuing controversy, Clarence Macartney's counter-attack was, appropriately enough, 'Shall Unbelief Win?'

In 1924 the Auburn Affirmation was signed by more than one thousand two hundred Presbyterian ministers. This document appeared to affirm both evangelical and liberal understandings of biblical infallibility, the virgin birth, substitutionary atonement, the resurrection, and miracles. It sounded orthodox, and seemed to breathe the air of good will to all men. But the liberal plea for tolerance was, as the unbeliever Walter Lippmann realized, tantamount to telling the evangelicals to 'smile and commit suicide'.

In 1925 John T. Scopes, a teacher in Dayton, Tennessee, confessed to teaching human evolution. William Jennings Bryan, a peace advocate who resigned as Woodrow Wilson's Secretary of State in 1915, regarded Darwinism as nothing more than 'guesses strung together', and thought that a believer in Darwinism might survive with his Christianity intact in the same way that some survive smallpox. Therefore, he prosecuted Scopes, who was defended by Clarence Darrow and the American Civil Liberties Union. Bryan won a victory of sorts, but the perception soon emerged that he had won the legal battle, but lost the war.

The movie *Inherit the Wind* (which was originally a play but was developed into a celluloid hoax) lauded the scientific sophistication of the evolutionists, despite the fact that in court they appealed to the recently discovered tooth of a possible missing link, 'Nebraska Man'. Two years after the trial, in 1927, it was found that Nebraska Man's tooth belonged to an extinct pig.

By 1926 the evangelical cause had been routed in the USA. The bastion of Reformed orthodoxy – the Theological Seminary at Princeton – was soon to be restructured so that it was shifted in a liberal direction. Whole denominations, such as the Presbyterian Church (USA), the United Methodist Church, the Episcopal Church, and the United Church of Christ, fled the 'Celestial City' to make their way towards the 'City of Destruction'. The Christian faith was first down-graded, and then Christian ethics were abandoned. By the end of the twentieth century, the Christian denominations had become virtually unrecognizable. This change is perhaps nowhere more clearly seen than in the continuing debates over the ordination of homosexuals to the Christian ministry.

5

NEO-ORTHODOXY

World War 1 was also the catalyst for the rise of what became known as neo-orthodoxy. During the War, the Swiss pastor Karl Barth (1886–1968) came to see the woeful inadequacy of the old optimistic liberalism, with its belief in human perfectibility and its portrayal of a gentle Jesus who taught people how to be loving and kind. Moral platitudes – such as Harnack's claim that Jesus taught the fatherhood of God, the brotherhood of man, and the infinite value of the human soul – had become irrelevant. H. R. Niebuhr was to mock the liberals: 'A God without wrath brought men without sin into a Kingdom without judgment through the ministrations of a Christ without a cross.'

Reacting to this, Barth turned to the Bible, and began to proclaim something like the old evangelical orthodoxy. This was crucial as the church confronted the threat of Nazism. At this time Barth revealed much courage and faithfulness. However, he retained his liberal belief in the fallibility of the Bible. To Barth, the infallible Word of God was Christ himself, not the Bible. He regarded the Bible as a human attempt to reproduce the Word of God. What he failed to grasp was that we can only know about Christ through the Bible.

The German theologian Rudolf Bultmann (1884–1976) also preached a kind of neo-orthodox gospel, interpreted in an existentialist way. But he retained far less of the Bible's history than Barth did. For example, he did not believe that we could know anything much about Jesus: 'I do indeed think that we can now know almost nothing concerning the life and personality of Jesus, since the early Christian sources show no interest in either, are moreover fragmentary and often legendary; and other sources about Jesus do not exist.' This sounds like an extreme version of the old liberalism, but Bultmann also preached that the evangelical gospel is existentially true, albeit historically false. To believe in the incarnation is not to believe that the Word became flesh and dwelt among us, but to hold to something that has next to nothing to do with history. In Bultmann's words: 'What matters is that the incarnation should not be conceived of as a miracle that happened about 1950 years ago, but as an eschatological happening, which, beginning with Jesus, is always present in the words of men proclaiming it to be a human experience.' He adds that 'the revelation has to be an event, which occurs whenever and wherever the word of grace is spoken to a man'. Naturally, Bultmann did not believe that Jesus actually rose from the dead. Nevertheless, he would preach that 'If a man accepts the word as directed to himself, as the word which offers to him death and life by means of death, he has believed in the Risen One.' This can be made to sound like the Christian faith but it is actually gobbledegook. It is believing in the *power* of the resurrection but not in *the resurrection itself*. It is faith standing not upon a rock but firmly in mid-air.

6

AFTER NEO-ORTHODOXY

Reaction to neo-orthodox irrationality led to a new 'quest for the historical Jesus', which began with Ernst Käsemann in 1953. This seemed to disappear from view in the 1970s. Existentialism had little interest in history, even in the kind of truncated history offered by the first two quests. But the 1980s saw the rise of the third quest, the most recent manifestation of this being the misnamed 'Jesus Seminar'. This is the brainchild of Robert Funk and his Westar Institute, basking in rather too much Californian sun. Funk and his colleagues do not regard the Gospels of Matthew, Mark and Luke as having much authority, or even as possessing some vague sense of reliability.

The Gospel of John has none at all, but the mis-named, apocryphal, and late (second century?) Gospel of Thomas is given considerable credence. The result is a Jesus without a story; all we have left are isolated, rather iconoclastic sayings. And there are not all that many of those. Were the Jesus Seminar to issue a 'Words of Christ in Red' edition of the Bible, it would be likely to be somewhat brief.

With an unerring grasp of what is likely to attract media attention in a biblically illiterate age, the 'scholars' of the Jesus Seminar devised a gimmick for publicizing what they regarded as the assured results of their deliberations. For each Gospel verse, a plastic bead was dropped into a bucket. Red indicated an authentic word from Jesus; pink indicated a probable word; grey was a sign of doubt; and black indicated the saying was not authentic. As a result, only 18 per cent of the words ascribed to Jesus in the Gospels are regarded as having been actually spoken by him.

Those who take this sort of thing seriously are informed that Jesus did say 'Blessed are the poor', but, alas, he did not say 'Blessed are the meek' or 'Blessed are the peacemakers'. Indeed, the vast majority of the Sermon on the Mount is eliminated, as is the blood atonement and the resurrection. The only saying from Mark's Gospel which is regarded as authentic is Mark 12:27, and only five of Jesus' parables are considered certain to go back to Jesus (*Matt.* 13:33; 20:1–15; *Luke* 10:30–35; 16:1–8), and the parable of the mustard seed as it is found in the apocryphal Gospel of Thomas.

The result is predictable enough. One of the Jesus Seminar participants, Hal Taussig, presents a Jesus who speaks of attaining global peace, inter-faith harmony, ecology and feminism. John Dominic Crossan portrays Jesus as a wandering revolutionary Cynic philosopher who was willing to have table fellowship with anyone and who opposed any hierarchical structure in any social grouping, including the family. There is no room, of course, for anything like a resurrection, so Crossan asserts that 'Christian faith is not Easter faith'.

Elisabeth Fiorenza portrays Jesus as one who saw God not as Father but as Sophia (the Greek goddess of wisdom). Hence this Jesus pitted himself against patriarchalism; he was thus a first century precursor of Fiorenza and the feminist gospel.

Some light relief is provided by Barbara Thiering who believes that Jesus married Mary Magdalene. Sadly, Mary proved to be the mad, unbelieving Rhoda of Acts 12 so Jesus divorced her. Later, he opened the heart of Lydia (*Acts* 16:14) and married her. The biblical claim that the word increased (*Acts* 6:7; 12:24) means that Jesus had children!

John Allegro has seriously suggested that Christianity derived from a sacred mushroom myth! Morton Smith wrote *Jesus the Magician* in 1978. Don Cupitt, using an image of Matthew Arnold's, wrote *The Sea of Faith* but what he taught was worthy of the title *Faith at Sea*. The plethora of such views in recent times has made it difficult to agree with A. A. Hodge's otherwise quite reasonable observation that 'Almost all heresies are partial truths – true in what they affirm, but false in what they deny.'

The formation of the World Council of Churches in 1948 gave hope to the liberals that their dream of a united church, armed with more liturgy than theology, might yet be realized. In 1956 the Presbyterian Church of the U.S.A. voted to ordain women, and twenty years later Letty Russell wrote a guide to a non-sexist interpretation of the Bible.

By 1970 R. P. C. Hanson was writing that 'the battle for the acceptance of historical criticism as applied to the Bible has been won.' In fact, it had been won – if that is the right word – well before then. In an oft-quoted expression, A. S. Peake had spoken at the turn of the twentieth century of the 'assured results' of higher criticism. In 1901 George

Adam Smith had boasted that 'Modern criticism has won its war against the traditional theories. It only remains to fix the amount of the indemnity.'

Throughout most of the twentieth century the majority of Protestant theological colleges in the Western world have been committed to some form of theological liberalism. This is especially noticeable in places where evangelicalism once held sway, notably Princeton Theological Seminary, and the Divinity Schools at Yale, Chicago and Duke Universities. The vast majority of leaders in the mainstream churches of Europe, North America, and Australia have adopted some form of liberalism.

The early liberals imbibed the confidence of their times. Towards the end of the nineteenth century, Marcus Dods exclaimed that 'the past fifty years have done more to promote the understanding of the New Testament than all the other Christian half-centuries put together'. In 1911 Albert Schweitzer asserted that, at the end of civilization, 'German theology will stand out as a great, a unique phenomenon in the mental and spiritual life of our time.' In fact, it has been greatly responsible for the spiritual ignorance and religious decay which ensued.

By and large the rationalism of the nineteenth century has given way to the arbitrary irrationalism of the twentieth and twenty-first centuries. William Robertson Smith spoke the language of evolutionary piety: 'All theology must advance, if only because the Christ of the gospels so far transcends the theology of any age that to cling to an unchangeable dogma is really to cease to look to Him whom we must ever seek to comprehend more fully, to love more singly, to follow more devotedly.'

The trouble was that faith was aiming at an ever-moving target, and devotion was separated from history. The boundaries were being moved; indeed, it was not clear that there could be any boundaries at all. Modernism rejects the notion of any *supernatural* truth; postmodernism rejects the notion of any *objective* truth. One leads into the morass of rationalism, the other into the mire of irrationalism. B. B. Warfield pointed to the solution to this dilemma when he wrote: 'We need the Jesus of history to account for the Christianity of history.'

7

KEY DOCTRINES

One needs to keep in mind that all the biblical doctrines are interconnected, so that denying one logically tends to pull the whole structure down. Leslie Weatherhead, for example, denied Jesus' miracles but not his resurrection. This seems rather like explaining Einstein's theory of relativity but failing to grasp the eight times table. However, because it is beyond the scope of this book to look exhaustively at all the major doctrines of the Christian faith, we will confine ourselves to six key doctrines.

SCRIPTURE

By definition, a liberal does not accept the full authority of Scripture. But the Bible claims that it was breathed out by God himself (2 *Tim.* 3:16). In the Old Testament, men moved by the Holy Spirit spoke from God (2 *Pet.* 1:21). Over four hundred times the Old Testament prophets declared: 'Thus says the LORD.' They were not giving their own opinions but making known the eternal word of the living God.

In the nineteenth century, liberal critics often claimed that writing was not invented till quite late, but this theory has been disproved. The Old Testament cannot be regarded as a collection of camp-fire stories which were embellished each time they were told. According to Judges 8:14 (NKJV, NIV, ESV, etc), even a boy could write.

From the beginning, the Old Testament Scriptures were progressively written down (e.g. *Gen.* 2:4; 5:1; 6:9; 10:1; 11:27; *Exod.* 24:4; *Deut.* 17:18; 31:9, 24–29; *Josh.* 24:26; *1 Sam.* 10:25; *1 Chron.* 29:29; *2 Chron.* 9:29; 12:15; 13:22; 20:34; 32:32; 33:18–19; *Isa.* 8:16; 30:8; *Jer.* 36:8, 10; *Dan.* 9:2; *Hab.* 2:2). So, for example, Daniel 9:2 refers to Jeremiah's prophecies while Jeremiah 26:18 cites Micah 3:12.

The New Testament speaks the same language of authority. To repulse the devil, Jesus quoted the Old Testament: 'It is written' (*Matt.* 4:4,7,10). He declared that the Scriptures could not be broken

(*John* 10:35) because God's word is truth (*John* 17:17). Jesus taught that heaven and earth would pass away but not his word (*Matt.* 24:35). The Apostle Paul regarded his gospel not as the word of man but the word of God (*1 Thess.* 2:13). Not to understand the Scriptures is to be in error (*Matt.* 22:29) for we must test all teaching by God's inerrant word (*Acts* 17:11).

To the liberal, the Bible is a book with errors in it, and only the scholars can say how many. Bishop Spong says: 'I love the Bible.' But he does not believe much of it. Emil Brunner accuses those who hold to the full authority of Scripture of 'making the Bible an idol and me its slave'. Marcus Dods was most outspoken, and declared that the doctrine of the verbal inspiration of Scripture was 'a theory which should be branded as heretical in every Christian Church'. Samuel Taylor Coleridge declared: 'That is inspired which inspires me.' But Scripture is inspired whether we are or not.

The evangelical does not claim to understand everything in the Bible. Augustine (A.D. 354–430) confessed that 'even in the Scriptures themselves the things which I do not know are many more than the things which I know'. In fact, even Daniel did not understand all that he had written (*Dan.* 12:8–9), and Peter did not find it easy to understand all that Paul wrote (2 *Pet.* 3:16).

Sometimes there are genuine doubts because of variations in the manuscripts. Textual criticism tries to find out what was originally written. One of the most important disputes concerns the last twelve verses of Mark's Gospel (*Mark* 16:9–20). Some faithful evangelical scholars believe that Mark wrote these words, but some do not. Either way, the authority of the Bible is not called into question. It is rather an issue of determining the content of the Bible. Such genuine matters of textual criticism need to be distinguished from the higher criticism of unbelieving and sceptical liberals.

The fact also has to be faced that there are some difficulties with the Bible. For example, Matthew records Jesus' temptations in the desert in an order different from Luke's record of the same event (*Matt.* 4:1–11 and *Luke* 4:1–13). One of the authors (if not both) was perhaps only interested in telling us what happened and not the strict chronology of what happened. Another problem concerns how Judas died. Matthew tells us that he hanged himself (*Matt.* 27:5) while Luke in Acts 1:18–19 rather enigmatically tells of how he fell headlong and his entrails gushed out. We may never be sure on this earth what happened exactly, but it may be that Judas hanged himself, then fell to the ground. Actually, there are remarkably few difficulties in the Bible, and suggestions made to harmonize biblical accounts are rather more credible than the wild hypotheses advanced in the name of scientific biblical criticism.

In fact, liberal criticism is far from being scientific; most of it is arbitrary and embarrassing. It was Bultmann who formulated the 'dissimilarity' principle – the rather silly rule which excludes any text which might have been spoken either by Jews or by Christians of the first century. Jesus is thus thought only to have said what could not have come from Judaism or the early church. There was no overlap at all. This nonsensical piece of pseudo-scientific reasoning would have devastating effects if applied to the reading of any daily newspaper.

If liberalism is true, the early church was enormously creative and uniquely stubborn. For example, because she was experiencing trials and tribulations, the church made up the story of Jesus stilling the storm. In this way she comforted herself with the notion that Jesus is Lord and so is present with his people and able to help them (*Mark* 4:35–41). We are meant to believe that the church made up stories about Jesus, and was then persecuted for believing them. Even more remarkable, these marvellous stories were created not by one genius but by a committee. Small wonder that in 1819 Richard Whately, in an ironic mood, wondered whether Napoleon existed.[1]

John Dominic Crossan tries to sound profound when he writes that 'he who finds meaning loses it, and he who loses it finds it'. This is self-defeating nonsense, and even a post-modernist cannot live with such a ludicrous notion. Presumably Crossan expected that his own books would be read and, hopefully, understood.

GOD

God reveals himself in the Bible as one God (*Deut.* 6:4; *James* 2:19) in three Persons – Father, Son, and Holy Spirit (*Matt.* 28:19–20). The Creator of the whole universe (*Gen.* 1:1) and the Judge of all the earth (*Gen.* 18:25), God is perfect (*Matt.* 5:48), holy (*Isa.* 6:3), unchanging (*Mal.*

---

[1] *Historical Doubts concerning Napoleon Bonaparte,* 1819. Whately's work was meant to show the absurdity of sceptical doubts about the historical existence of Jesus and the authenticity of the Gospels.

3:6), eternal (*Exod.* 3:14; *Psa.* 90:2), all-know-ing (*Jer.* 17:10), everywhere-present (*Jer.* 23:24), and all-powerful (*Psa.* 115:3). He is loving and merciful, and he is righteous and just – attributes which are especially revealed in Christ's death at Calvary. Here Christ satisfied the justice of the Father, and here mercy is extended to sinners. Here, and nowhere else, and in no other way.

Liberals do not accept this view of God. Paul Tillich (1886–1965) wrote, 'He who knows about depth knows about God.' God was not a personal being to whom one prayed but 'the ground of being' about which one meditated. John A. T. Robinson (1919-1983; Anglican Bishop of Woolwich) thought similarly, and taught that God is 'ultimate reality'.

Interestingly enough, the Cambridge physicist Stephen Hawking also speaks of the existence of God, but only an impersonal God. Wisdom can-not be equated with intellect, for in all areas of life, personality ranks higher than impersonality. For example, a dog ranks higher than a stone. Yet Hawk-ing would have us believe that the highest being is impersonal.

These days it is common to hear people refer, with David Jenkins (a former Anglican Bishop of Dur-ham), to a 'He/She God'. Clark Pinnock too thinks that God may perhaps be addressed as 'mother'. In the 1960s there were even theologians who proclaimed the 'death of God'. Embracing a theology known as 'Open Theism', Clark Pinnock and John Sanders have begun to write of a God who is not omniscient. This God apparently knows more than we do, but does not know everything. Presumably, this would make prophecy somewhat hazardous. Indeed, God can even change his mind. The only thing that we can be sure of about him is that he (or she) is love. This view grew out of 'Process Theology', which told of a God who is evolving, along with everything else.

THE PERSON OF CHRIST

In the liberal view, Jesus was a Palestinian peasant who somehow was mistaken for God incarnate by his strictly monotheistic followers. It is now common to say, as does Frances Young, that the New Testament has many Christologies. Jesus is usually portrayed as the fairest flower of humanity, a man particularly favoured by God. Ritschl thought that Christ has the value of God for us. Michael Goulder even blames Simon Magus (*Acts* 8) for introducing what he calls 'incarnational speculations' into the church!

By contrast, the Christ of the Bible is the one in whom the fullness of the deity dwells bodily (*Col.* 2:9). He is thus truly God and truly man in the one Person. He declared himself to be one with the Father (*John* 10:30), and accepted the worship of Thomas when he acknowledged him as his Lord and God (*John* 20:28). He identified himself as the King in God's kingdom (*Matt.* 25:31–46), the one who would raise the dead and judge the whole world (*John* 5:28–29), and the one who could forgive sins (*Mark* 2:1–12). As the Son of God, he is equal with God (*John* 5:18). To the Jews, he spoke of himself in the same terms as Jehovah: 'Before Abraham was, I am' (*John* 8:58). Those who did not believe him regarded him as a blasphemer (for example, *John* 8:59; *Matt.* 26:65).

Christ is worshipped (for example, *Matt.* 2:11; 28:17; *John* 9:35–38), although angels are not (*Col.* 2:18; *Rev.* 19:10; 22:8–9). Barbara Thiering simply misses the point when she writes: 'Jesus, a man who lived in Israel two thousand years ago, was someone whom I admire very much, for what he did politically. But I will not worship a human being. And I do not believe in the virgin birth. I do not think it is religious to do violence to your intelligence.' Christ never calls us to admire him as a great man; he calls us to bow before him as Lord. As Charles Lamb put it: 'If Shakespeare entered we should all rise; if He (that is, Christ) appeared, we must kneel.'

The great Russian novelist Fyodor Dostoyevsky once said that it was virtually impossible for a novelist to portray perfection in a realistic way. Yet in Christ we have perfection and reality in one. He is what I am and also what I am not. He is fully man, one who was hungry and thirsty, who slept, who wept, who suffered, and who died. But he never sinned (*Heb.* 7:26). Yet he is not the 'white knight on the horse' of the fairytale; he is historically true.

The atheist John Stuart Mill (who did finally come to think that there was some probability that some kind of God did exist) praised Jesus as 'probably the greatest moral reformer and martyr to that mission who ever existed upon earth'. That is essentially the liberal view of Jesus. It sounds as if it is on the right track, but in fact it betrays a failure to think clearly. Practically everything that Jesus said was an indirect claim to deity. If he was wrong, his error was truly monumental, of gigantic proportions, and the Sermon on the Mount, for example, would have to be discarded as the product of a diseased mind.

Regarding the liberal view of Christ, John Gresham Machen (1881–1937) asked:

What shall be thought of a human being who lapsed so far from the path of humility and sanity as to believe that the eternal destinies of the world were committed into His hands?

It is a well-made point. Because of the claims he made for himself, if Christ be not God, he cannot be good.

SALVATION

Liberals tend to be optimistic about human nature. The vast majority believe in evolution, and the doctrine of the Fall of man is treated as something that is not literally true. The notion of propitiation – that Christ's death satisfies the holy justice of God the Father – is one which the liberal mind finds especially offensive. John McLeod Campbell (1800–72), a Scottish minister, was one of the first to move towards softening what he saw as the harsh evangelical doctrine of salvation. To the liberal, God is *loving;* to the evangelical, God is *both loving and just.*

Scripture teaches that because sin is in all people everywhere (*Rom.* 3:9–10), God's wrath against all ungodliness and unrighteousness of men (*Rom.* 1:18) rests on all. We are by nature 'children of wrath' (*Eph.* 2:3). Hence the human condition is this: 'Whoever believes in the Son has eternal life; whoever does not obey the Son shall not see life, but the wrath of God remains on him' (*John* 3:36).

The purpose of Christ's death on the cross was to pay the penalty for sin. In sending his Son to die, the Father was showing himself both just and the justifier of guilty sinners who believe in Jesus (*Rom.* 3:25–26). At Calvary, God demonstrates both his mercy and his justice. He punishes sin as it deserves and offers mercy to all who believe the gospel. Christ bore God's wrath in our place and so became a curse for us (*Gal.* 3:13). He who knew no sin was made to be sin for us (2 *Cor.* 5:21). All this is anathema to the liberal, who tends to think that God should just let bygones be bygones. The answer to that way of thinking is the same as that given by Anselm of Canterbury in the eleventh century: 'You have not yet considered the weight of sin.'

The older liberals were usually quite moralistic and saw salvation in terms of living up to the 'Golden Rule' of doing to others as you would have them do to you (*Matt.* 7:12). Harnack, for example, applauded the early church for her opposition to the widespread practice of abortion under the Roman

Empire. In the liberal scheme of things, Christ's death is meant to melt our hearts and cause us to turn back to God. Our repentance – not Christ's death – becomes the basis for our acceptance with God. The American Congregationalist Horace Bushnell (1802–76) was one who popularized this view.

That most Victorian of men Leslie Stephen (who solemnly renounced his Anglican orders in 1875, after having lost his faith) wrote: 'I now believe in nothing, to put it shortly; but I do not the less believe in morality . . . I mean to live and die like a gentleman if possible.' For many in the late nineteenth and early twentieth centuries, faith was replaced by moralism. The fiercely anti-Christian philosopher, Friedrich Nietzsche, lampooned the 'English flatheads' who thought that they could have morality without faith. How prophetic his words have proved to be!

Modern liberals are usually far less concerned with traditional Christian moral teachings. Having long ago abandoned Christian doctrine, they feel no compunction about abandoning Christian ethics too. So, for example, Bishop Spong teaches that love is unconditional, and the church 'must be broken open and freed of its noninclusive prejudices. That is why slavery, segregation, sexism, bigotry, and homophobia tear at the very soul of the church.'

It has now become fashionable to take the side of Sodom and Gomorrah.

The rise of 'Liberation Theology' came to an abrupt halt when Marxism collapsed with the fall of the Berlin Wall in 1989. While it lasted, Liberation Theology portrayed salvation as redemption from economic and social oppression rather than from sin. Feminist theologians have continued this kind of approach with their attempts to portray salvation as release from patriarchal prejudice. Special pleading is never a convincing way of studying the Word of God.

Many, perhaps most, modern liberals are universalists. They believe that everyone is going to be saved in the end. There is a dislike of portraying God as the Judge of all the earth. The popular liberal evangelical-sounding commentator, William Barclay, for example, came to believe that everybody on earth would ultimately go to heaven. Against this, Christ taught that two groups of people will appear before God – the saved and the condemned (*John* 5:28–29), those inside the kingdom and those outside (*Matt.* 8:11–12), good fish and bad fish (*Matt.* 13:47–50), the sheep and the goats (*Matt.* 25:31–46), and those who were ready for his coming and those who were not (*Matt.* 25:1–13). Christ will cause some to rise and others to fall (*Luke* 2:34). The gospel message will be the fragrance of life to those who are being saved and the smell of death to those who are perishing (2 *Cor.* 2:15–16).

Clark Pinnock and John Sanders believe that a person can be saved by seeing God through his or her conscience or by marvelling at the beauties of nature. According to this view, the gardener amongst her roses or the surfer out amongst the waves may appreciate something of nature, and so be made right with God.

Michael Ramsey, a former Archbishop of Canterbury, declared in 1961: 'Heaven is not a place for Christians only . . . I expect to see some present-day atheists there.' Later, Billy Graham appeared to express similar sentiments.

The Scriptures, on the other hand, say that there is only one mediator between God and men (*1 Tim.* 2:5). The apostolic message is that there is salvation in no-one other than Jesus Christ (*Acts* 4:12). Our Lord declared quite plainly: 'I am the way, and the truth, and the life. No one comes to the Father except through me' (*John* 14:6).

Flying in the face of biblical truth, Pope John Paul 11 twice held inter-faith prayer meetings at Assisi to pray for world peace.

THE RESURRECTION OF CHRIST

In the middle of the second century A.D., one of the early church Fathers, Justin Martyr, told of what Christians did when they met together on the first day of the week. Justin says that the service of worship consisted of readings from Scripture, exhortation, prayer, the Lord's Supper, and a collection for the orphans and widows. The extraordinary thing is that a religion which regarded the Old Testament as its foundation and starting point set aside Sunday for weekly worship rather than Saturday, the traditional Jewish day of rest. What led to the change of day? The answer is the resurrection of Jesus Christ on the 'first day of the week'. In the Old Testament, believers were to celebrate the conclusion of the old creation; in the New Testament, believers are to celebrate the beginning of the new creation.

Unbelievers, whether religious or irreligious, tend to portray the Christian faith as an assault on reason. The Romantic poet, Shelley, for example, declared, 'All religious notions are founded solely on authority; all the religions of the world forbid examination and do not want one to reason.' But the Apostle Paul faced facts – if Christ did not rise from the dead, then Christians were of all men to be pitied (*1 Cor.* 15:19).

It is the liberal mind that is reluctant to confront reality. David Jenkins claimed to believe 'passionately' in the resurrection of Christ, although he was also widely reported to have referred to it as 'a conjuring trick with bones'. 'The question is', as Alice put it to Humpty Dumpty, 'whether you can make words mean so many different things.' Without the literal physical resurrection of Jesus, there would be a gaping and inexplicable hole left in the history of Jesus and the rise of the early church.

When it comes to the central tenet of the resurrection of Christ, Bishop Spong and John Dominic Crossan both claim that the resurrection stories were legends which simply grew. Barbara Thiering believes that Jesus never died on the cross, so there is no place for a resurrection. Sometimes one is even treated to an exercise in logic: 'All men are mortal. Jesus is a man. Therefore Jesus is mortal.'

This kind of thing is presumably meant to leave orthodox Christians floundering in the wake of such advanced scientific thinking! Actually, the problem today is not so much that the evidence has been examined and found wanting, but that it has not been examined in the first place. One could only wish there was more hard thinking, not less. J. B. Phillips was right to complain that 'the most important Event in human history is politely and quietly by-passed'.

How, then, do we tackle the hard facts of the claim that in the third decade of the first century A.D. a man, Jesus of Nazareth, died on a Roman cross, but within three days rose from the dead, never to die again?

The first thing to note is that the documents which make this claim are consistent with themselves. This is not to say that there are not a few difficulties. For example, all four Gospels tell us that it was the women who first made their way to Jesus' tomb on that fateful Sunday, but Luke seems to mention at least five women (*Luke* 24:10), Mark, three (*Mark* 16:1), Matthew, two (*Matt.* 28:1), while John only mentions Mary Magdalene (*John* 20:1). An explanation would satisfy our curiosity, but the difficulty hardly represents an internal contradiction. After all, if there were five, there was also one; and if there was one, there could also have been five. John, for instance, does not say that there was *only* one. In fact, the 'we' in John 20:2 indicates that Mary was not alone.

One should also point out that the resurrection of Jesus was not something which took place in a corner. All in all, there were probably at least twelve appearances of the resurrected Jesus over a forty-day period. Well over five hundred men, not counting the women, saw Jesus after he rose from the dead (see *1 Cor.* 15:3–8). Scripture requires two or more witnesses to record a conviction in law (*Deut.* 19:15). The resurrection of Jesus amply fulfils this requirement!

The Old Testament itself had prophesied that the suffering servant would be vindicated (*Isa.* 53:1–9, 10–12) and that the one forsaken by God (*Psa.* 22:1–21) would rule to the ends of the earth (*Psa.* 22:21–31; see *Psa.* 16:8–11).

Jesus too prophesied not only his death but his resurrection from the dead (*Matt.* 16:21; 17:9, 22–23; 20:18–19). Jesus never presented himself as simply a mortal man, even an extraordinary mortal man. Consistently he portrayed himself as the Lord from heaven, the eternal Son of the eternal Father, who brings something of the glory of heaven to earth, veiled though it was in some respects. Jesus Christ is indeed the resurrection and the life (*John* 11:25).

The narrow-minded, even bigoted, unbeliever needs to explain some hard facts. Why could nobody produce the dead body of Jesus? The authorities had every reason to produce it if they could, for Christianity could have been crushed in its infancy by the public display of Jesus' corpse. In spite of the fact that dead bodies are notoriously difficult to conceal, the authorities were not able to find it. The tomb was empty because Jesus arose from the dead.

Also, what transformed the apostles from the fearful band who met on the Thursday night for the Last Supper to the fearless band which went out preaching Christ risen in the hostile environment of Jerusalem? Something – or someone – got a hold of them and radically transformed them.

Peter had denied Christ three times (*Mark* 14:66–72), but in Acts 2–5 the same man risks his life to declare that Jesus is the Christ, and that the great proof of this is his rising from the grave. The obvious explanation lies in the fact that Peter (and the others) were convinced that Jesus was alive again.

This was certainly not the result of wishful thinking. In spite of all the prophecies, none of the disciples expected Jesus to rise from the dead (*Matt.* 28:17; *Luke* 24:11, 21, 25, 37; *John* 20:15, 24–28; 21:4). It was not a case of only one 'doubting Thomas'; they all doubted.

Mary Magdalene, for example, saw the risen Christ and thought he must be the gardener; she did not see the gardener and think that he must be Jesus risen from the dead!

Those who are determined not to follow the apostolic evidence wherever it leads have a hard time of it. Hermann Samuel Reimarus in 1778 claimed that the disciples did not want to return to their old jobs, so they stole Jesus' body, waited fifty days, and then proclaimed the resurrection. One of the troubles with this conspiracy theory is that it was the disciples' belief that Jesus had triumphed bodily over the grave that led to the persecution of Christians. Fishing may not have been Reimarus' idea of the ultimate way of life, but it is surely more appealing than being flogged, stoned, thrown to wild beasts, or crucified! Ten men were unable to keep the Watergate conspiracy secret for two weeks before the truth emerged. Human beings may be prepared to suffer for a lie that they do not know is a lie. Hence communism has its 'martyrs'. But nobody will die for something which he knows is fraudulent.

As for the explanation that the women went to the wrong tomb, that is rather like trying to explain Hiroshima by postulating some juvenile misuse of fireworks.

We can pretend that these things are not true. Eugene Christian once wrote a book entitled, *How to*

Live to Be a Hundred. Alas, he died at 69, although that is not the greatest tragedy of his life. The Christian lives with eternity in view.

In April 1945 the Lutheran theologian Dietrich Bonhoeffer was led off to be tried and then executed by the Nazis. Before he was taken away, he told one British prisoner to tell his friend, Bishop George Bell of Chichester, 'For me it is the end, but also the beginning.' The resurrection of Christ is, for the Christian believer, victory over the last enemy, death itself.

HEAVEN AND HELL

The humanist Julian Huxley argued that man created the gods to protect himself from loneliness, uncertainty and fear. If that is the case, it is hard to explain why men thought up the doctrine of everlasting punishment. Darwin himself objected to hell as 'a damnable doctrine', and this played its part in his postulating the hypothesis of evolution. The same kind of attitude can also be found in the church. C. H. Dodd, for example, objected to any concept of 'the wrath of God'.

Scripture tells us plainly about two final places – heaven and hell (for example in *Psa.* 73:25–28). But it is Christ himself who tells us most about heaven and hell. Since he is the only one who has come down from heaven, he is better qualified than any liberal critic to tell us what heaven is like (*John* 3:13). It is also Jesus who tells us about hell, that it is the place of outer darkness, where there is weeping and gnashing of teeth (*Matt.* 8:12; 13:42, 50), an everlasting fire (*Matt.* 25:41), and unending torments, and that there is an unbridgeable gulf between the saved and the damned (*Luke* 16:22–26).

In the new heaven and new earth, there will be no more sin, nor sorrow, nor death (*Rev.* 21:3–4); but in the judgment there will only be the sorrow and pain of the second death (*Rev.* 20:10; 21:8). One place tells of joy and love beyond anything we have ever experienced; the other tells of misery beyond anything we have suffered on earth.

Evangelicals shy away from the notion that all shall be saved, but there have been many who have wished to soften the doctrine of everlasting punishment. The idea that unbelievers will be annihilated rather than suffer the eternal pains of hell has been advocated by many evangelicals, including John Stott, John Wenham, Michael Green, Stephen Travis, and Philip Edgcumbe Hughes. It is clear, however that the Bible does not refer to a state of non-existence. The rich man suffers in hell (*Luke* 16:19–31). Jesus says of Judas that it would have been good for that man if he had not been born (*Matt.* 26:24). That can hardly be true unless there is a place of everlasting punishment (see too *Deut.* 32:22; *Psa.* 11:6; *Isa.* 66:24; *Matt.* 8:12; 18:8–9; 25:30, 41, 46; *Mark* 9:42-48; *Rom.* 2:3–9; *Heb.* 6:2; 10:27, 29; *Rev.* 14:11; 21:8).

It is fair to say that scholarly rejection of the notion of everlasting judgment has next to nothing to do with any attempt at objective biblical criticism. It is simply a case of moral horror that God could fail to take a respectable place at the round table of relativism, and instead claim to be the Judge of all the earth.

8

HOW SHOULD A CHRISTIAN RESPOND TO THEOLOGICAL LIBERALISM?

George Carey, Archbishop of Canterbury from 1991 to 2002, says of the Church of England:

> I remain convinced it is a broad Church combining the catholic, evangelical, charismatic and liberal in joyful harmony . . . For many of us in the Church, liberalism is a creative and constructive element for exploring theology today . . . It would constitute the end of Anglicanism as a significant force in worldwide Christianity if we lost this ingredient.

The same kind of approach is found in other pro-
fessedly evangelical circles – for example, in the
editorial of the evangelical magazine, *Themelios*,
for October–November 1988 where it is urged that
liberals be regarded as Christian brothers and sisters. On this view, liberal Christianity is a valid and
authentic, if somewhat wayward, form of Christianity. Liberals are thus to be accepted as part of God's
family. A family might squabble occasionally, but it
is still family.

In 1881, the Scottish evangelical Alexander Whyte
showed a similar attitude when he defended William
Robertson Smith. He asserted, 'I find no disparity,
no difficulty, in carrying much of the best of our
past with me in going out to meet and hail the new
theological methods.'

Whyte accepted at face value the claim that
Robertson Smith was a believing critic. It was a naïve
stance. In reality, the churches were – to cite P. T.
Forsyth's metaphor – like picnickers on the slopes of
a temporarily dormant volcano.

J. Gresham Machen opposed this accommodating
view of liberalism. In 1923 he published his clarion
call, *Christianity and Liberalism*. This was a lucid and
devastating attack on theological liberalism, which
he treated as another religion: 'Naturalistic liberal-

ism is not Christianity at all.' Hence he considered that separation was 'the crying need of the hour'. Those who saw themselves as orthodox evangelicals but who treated liberals as true Christians were especially warned by Machen that it was an either/or matter. Christianity and theological liberalism were in direct opposition to one another. It was not just a matter of which doctrinal system one adhered to, but of how one regarded denials of that system. The importance of doctrine itself was at stake: 'It concerns the question not of this doctrine or that, but of the importance which is attributed to doctrine as such.'

Francis Schaeffer called the evangelical wavering on basic issues *The Great Evangelical Disaster*. Schaeffer's cry was uttered in the spirit of Elijah – if Baal is God, worship him; if the LORD is God, worship him (*1 Kings* 18:21). C. S. Lewis too came to see the dangers of what he called 'Christianity and water'. He warned: 'Liberal Christianity can only supply an ineffectual echo to the massive chorus of agreed and admitted unbelief.' Some individual liberals may grasp enough of the gospel to be saved – even the hem of Christ's garment can heal – but liberalism as such is an assault on the gospel. It ought to be regarded as a form of unbelief.

One of the most remarkable conversions in recent times is that of Eta Linnemann.[1] She was Honorary Professor of New Testament at Philipps University, Marburg, Germany, and a disciple of Bultmann when she came to saving faith in Christ. In 1978 she threw all of her writings out with the trash. Her views now are: 'In the same way that I resist adultery in the name of Jesus, I can also resist historical-critical theology.' Christian theology and liberal theology are as contrary to one another as Christianity and sin.

To reject the Bible is to reject God's revelation of himself, and so to reject God. In 1841 John Henry Newman referred to liberalism as 'the characteristic of the destined Antichrist'. Certainly, it is idolatrous because it rejects God as he has made himself known, and in his place constructs a god who is a product of the liberals' own imagination. In essence, liberal Christianity belongs with the cults.

Christians must be prepared to identify liberals, and to name names if necessary (*Rom.* 16:17–18; *2 Tim.* 2:17–18). We are not to have fellowship with such people and make-believe that they are Christians (*2 Thess.* 3:6, 14; *2 John* 10). If they will not embrace the biblical faith, they need to be disciplined (*1 Cor.*

[1] Her testimony, and other short addresses by Dr Linnemann, can be found at www.gracevalley.org.

5; *Rev.* 2:20–21). Wheat and tares may look alike, but wheat and Parramatta grass do not.[1]

Yet it is not enough to bemoan the situation or denounce liberal 'Christians'. Francis Schaeffer found a rather repellent ferocity of spirit amongst separatist American Presbyterians after the divisions of the 1930s. The truth needs to be declared, but it needs to be declared in a right and godly spirit. As he contemplated the enemies of the cross in his day, Paul wept (*Phil.* 3:18). We have no biblical warrant to be harsh and hyper-critical. Our love is to abound more and more in knowledge and all discernment (*Phil.* 1:9).

Often the shift away from the faith once delivered can be quite subtle at first, and true Christians may not be aware that they have given away precious ground. It is altogether too easy both to over-react and to under-react. There are dangers on all sides. If we are Christians, we must speak the truth in love (*Eph.* 4:15) – both truth and love are equally necessary. No matter what our denomination, we must not compromise and we must maintain fellowship with all true Christians.

The issue of liberal theology is not a minor one, but a matter of life and death, of the destiny of immortal

---

[1] A troublesome coarse weed, difficult to eradicate, found in pasture land in Australia.

souls. Marcus Dods, the Free Church Professor of New Testament at New College, Edinburgh, wrote glowingly in 1889, 'It might be difficult to lay one's finger on any half-century in the world's history during which changes so rapid, so profound, so fruitful, and so permanent have taken place as those which the past generation has seen.' Yet in his later years Dods wrote gloomily to a correspondent

> One who can believe in God should be very thankful. Very often, I may say commonly, I cannot get further than the conviction that in Christ we see the best that our nature is capable of, and must make that our own.

Unbelief has led to despair. But Christ is the one who has defeated death, and is alive for evermore.

Francis Schaeffer put on record his last meeting with Jim Pike, an Episcopalian bishop who was well-known for his liberal views on doctrine and ethics. In fact, the bishop's son had committed suicide, and Pike tried to communicate with him through a medium (contrary to God's law in *Deut.* 18:10–11). Pike told Schaeffer:

> When I turned from being agnostic, I went to Union Theological Seminary, eager for and expecting

bread; but when I graduated, all that it left me was a handful of pebbles.

Liberal theology offers us a handful of pebbles; the God of the Bible offers us Jesus Christ – 'the Bread of life'.

FOR FURTHER READING

ETA LINNEMANN *Historical Criticism of the Bible: Methodology or Ideology?* Translated by Robert W. Yarbrough (Grand Rapids: Kregel, 2001).

J. GRESHAM MACHEN *Christianity and Liberalism* (Grand Rapid: Eerdmans, 1923; often reprinted).

IAIN H. MURRAY *Evangelicalism Divided: A Record of Crucial Change in the Years 1950–2000* (Edinburgh: Banner of Truth, 2000).

FRANCIS SCHAEFFER *The Great Evangelical Disaster* (Wheaton: Crossway Books, 1984).

INDEX OF NAMES

Index of Names